I WITNESS

LIVING INSIDE THE STORIES *of* ADVENT & CHRISTMAS

ISBN: 978-0-88028-452-3

Forward
Movement

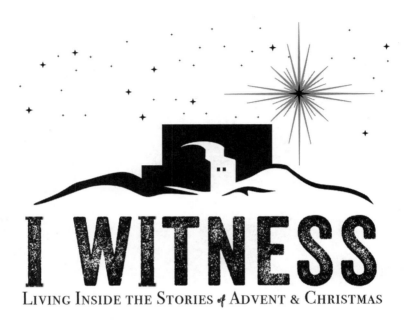

I WITNESS

LIVING INSIDE THE STORIES *of* ADVENT & CHRISTMAS

Kate Moorehead

Forward Movement

Cincinnati, Ohio

Introduction

When I was a little girl, I got lost inside stories. My mom was a composer and a concert pianist, and she stayed at home with me and my brother. She gave us the gift of unstructured time, and my imagination filled in the empty spaces. I lay under the piano as she played, imagining I was shipwrecked on an island. I spent entire weeks making forts for my dolls with elaborate plots of rescue and intrigue. My world was huge within the confines of our house on Willow Street in New Haven, Connecticut.

As I grew older, my mom started writing small operas to be performed in churches in place of the sermon. She called them chancel operas as they were sung in the chancel—the space around the altar. Since there was no budget, casting was sometimes a challenge, and I played Mary many times. I also played the angel Gabriel, the unnamed disciple on the road to Emmaus, and other roles suitable for a young woman. Within these operas, I lived the stories again.

When Jesus tells us that we must be like little children to enter the kingdom of heaven, he must be referring, at least in part, to the imagination of a child. A child doesn't just read a story: A child enters a story, lives within it, and explores every nook and crevice. Imagination is a sign not only of creativity but also of a child's sense of safety. When I worked in orphanages in Russia, I quickly noticed that the children did not play imaginary games. They hardly played at all. It was as if they were tiny adults, too afraid of what might happen in the real world to risk imagining another. When I traveled to Maine to see how two girls from the orphanage were adjusting to their new adoptive home, the first thing I noticed was that they had begun to play and dream. This was a great sign, for it meant that they were beginning to feel safe.

If we are to draw closer to God, we must enter the story of salvation as a child, with our hearts and minds wide open. We must be willing to enter the story and live within it, imagining ourselves within the skin of the people of God. We must be there with Jesus on the night he is born.

Most of us have heard the story of Jesus' birth many, many times. But have you lived inside it? In the sixteenth century, Saint Ignatius tried to teach us what children do naturally. He urged us to live within the great story and to experience it from the inside. This book is an attempt to do just that.

This Advent and Christmas, let us live within the story of the birth of our Savior.

Kate Moorehead
Saint Mary the Virgin

Editor's Note: This book contains reflections for the full four weeks of Advent and the twelve days of Christmas. Of course, the Advent season lasts a different number of days each year, depending on the day of the week of Christmas. If you are reading this book during a year in which Christmas Day falls earlier in the fourth week of Advent, simply skip ahead to the devotion for Christmas Day (or double up and read extra meditations!).

As a tool to bring you into the stories, we use present tense. When we are with God, it really is right now, this moment. It is I AM, not I was.

First Sunday of Advent
Waiting for God

In the days of King Herod of Judea, there was a priest named Zechariah, who belonged to the priestly order of Abijah. His wife was a descendant of Aaron, and her name was Elizabeth. Both of them were righteous before God, living blamelessly according to all the commandments and regulations of the Lord. But they had no children, because Elizabeth was barren, and both were getting on in years.

Luke 1:5-7

The name Zechariah in Hebrew means *The Lord has remembered*. Zechariah has prayed for a lifetime. He has prayed to have a son, and God has not answered his prayers. He must think God has forgotten him. He must think God has not remembered.

Imagine what it must feel like to worship every day in the temple, to hear the prayers of thousands of pilgrims—and to hear rejoicing from many of the pilgrims as their prayers are answered. Meanwhile, no answer comes for you. Does Zechariah feel like a hypocrite? Does he begin to doubt the existence of God? Does he wonder if God is listening at all? Does he think that God has forgotten him?

Sons are more precious than gold in biblical times. To have a son is to carry on your bloodline. To remain barren is to experience a kind of social shame, a premature death, a deep and profound loneliness. Without sons, a man is lost. There is no future life beyond his death. He is alone.

Only one priest is chosen each year to go into the Holy of Holies. We don't know if Zechariah has ever been chosen before but we do know that he is selected as an old man to go inside this holiest place on earth for Jews. I wonder if he thinks that this is his one and only chance to ask God for a son. I wonder: Does a spark of hope ignite within his soul or has that spark long since gone out?

Do his knees hurt as he kneels in that holiest of places? Does he weep for sorrow at his lost hope? Does he look down on his wrinkled hands and believe that it is too late?

As Zechariah enters a new place, God finally responds. Zechariah's prayers are answered. The Lord has remembered.

When we pray, it is hard to wait for an answer. We expect results from God, like fast-food prayers, on our timeline, as ordered, but often those results don't come. Zechariah has waited a lifetime. He has asked God for a son time and again for his entire adult life, and the answer does not come until he is an old man, long past believing he would ever become a father. But the answer does come. The answer finally comes.

Jesus later teaches that anyone who asks receives from God, and I believe his words are true. But the variable is time. When will our prayers be answered? If we are willing to wait like Zechariah, we will see the day when God responds, when God remembers.

Have you asked God for something? Are you still waiting for an answer? Advent is the season of waiting. Join Zechariah in waiting for God to come.

First Monday of Advent
Awareness

*Once when he was serving as priest before God
and his section was on duty, he was chosen by lot,
according to the custom of the priesthood, to enter the
sanctuary of the Lord and offer incense.*

Luke 1:8-9

When you enter a room, do you expect to see God? Most
of us don't think twice before walking from one room to
another. We move unconsciously, following rote patterns,
our minds distracted. If we were truly alert and aware, we
would search for God around every corner. Imagine what
we might find if we stayed awake—ever watchful of who
we might meet and what we might discover.

When Zechariah walks into the Holy of Holies, he is wide
awake. He is there to light incense. This is his job. The
space must be majestic, awe-inspiring. It is so rare to enter
this space; most Israelites will never have the privilege.
His old eyes are wide open, witnessing the beauty many

will never be blessed to see. Even though it is his job and a relatively mundane task, Zechariah is prepared to see something extraordinary.

And he does: an angel.

A question keeps me awake at night: Does the angel only appear to Zechariah or do angels appear to all of us and only people like Zechariah are able to see them? In other words, does the vision of an angel depend on our merit or on our state of awareness?

What if angels appear in front of all of us every day, all day, but we are too asleep or too blind or too distracted to see them? What if they are right around the corner? In the next room? If Zechariah had been thinking about dinner or the next day's chores, would he still have encountered the angel? Is Zechariah's state of awareness—his anticipation of seeing something extraordinary—what enables him to see and recognize the angel?

Many of us feel like the gears of our brains are running on overtime. But just because we are active and thinking doesn't mean we are cultivating awareness. In fact, it seems that the busier our minds become, the less we are aware of our surroundings. Being truly present and awake takes a lot of focus. It takes practice and meditation. We may be using our entire brains when we go about our daily lives, but we are not using them to their fullest capacity.

Jesus will later tell us that the kingdom of heaven is near. It is, in fact, all around us. How can we cultivate the awareness of heaven itself? How can we see it more clearly?

The Hindu saint Ramakrishna put it this way, "Don't seek God, SEE God."

Imagine the state of Zechariah's awareness when he walks through the doors and into the room that is called the Holy of Holies. Imagine his eyes wide open, his mind alert, his heart open. Let us try to cultivate the same kind of awareness as Zechariah as the door opens and he sees the angel.

How can you become more awake each moment? What are some practices that you could adopt to cultivate awareness?

First Tuesday of Advent
Gathering to Pray with Others

*Now at the time of the incense offering, the whole
assembly of the people was praying outside.*
Luke 1:10

When a priest is chosen to enter the Holy of Holies,
the people gather outside and pray. Their presence is
considered part of the journey into the Holy of Holies.
One man walks inside while a whole group of priests and
people pray outside. The Levites will never send a priest
into the Holy of Holies alone without a community behind
him, praying for him.

How much is Zechariah's encounter with the angel
influenced by the crowd of people who are praying for him
at the time? And how much are our lives influenced by the
prayers of others?

A few years ago, I went to the hospital early in the
morning to pray for a woman awaiting surgery for breast

cancer. I found myself sitting in a waiting room with three other women: a Congregationalist minister, a woman who led a small church in the inner city, and the wife of a retired bishop. Without discussion, we joined hands and began to pray.

A sudden, almost electric presence entered the room when we prayed. It was different than the presence of God that I have felt on my own, different and yet the same. There was a potency in our coming together, a strength in our shared words and joined hands.

I left the hospital that day convinced that I needed to meet with these women again. Whatever happened when we prayed, I needed to happen again. I felt like I had plugged into an electrical socket and the Holy Spirit was coursing through me. I knew that I must find these women again.

I sent them all an email. *Could we pray together, regularly?* To my surprise, they all said yes, and we began to pray together every week. And the prayers have changed me. Sometimes they have been answered and sometimes I'm still waiting for a response, but I have been changed because being in the presence of these praying women is being in God's presence.

Jesus says that when two or three are gathered, God will be in the midst of them. Does this mean God is not present when we are alone? Of course not. God is with us always, inside us and around us. But there is a power when people gather for the express purpose of prayer. It makes a difference.

When Zechariah walks into the sacred room, a group of people are praying for him. They are speaking words and thinking about his experience and asking God to be present. And their prayers make a difference: A great prophet is conceived.

Do you pray regularly with a small group of people? Why or why not? What impact could this have on your life?

First Wednesday of Advent
Gratitude

His wife was a descendant of Aaron, and her name was Elizabeth.

Luke 1:5b

She is a daughter of Aaron. A woman of the best breeding. A vessel for bearing priestly sons. As a young girl, she must have been highly sought after, given that she was such quality marriage material. To marry Elizabeth would unite a man to the line of Aaron, Moses' brother, the great priest who led the people of God from slavery to freedom. Elizabeth is highly regarded by God and her sole purpose is to bear sons, to carry on the priestly line.

And then no sons come. No children at all. Imagine if your entire value as a person rested on the one thing you could not seem to do. With no understanding of infertility issues, the inability to bear children is seen as a failure of the woman. It is a judgment upon her, a sign that she is out of favor with God.

Every month, when Elizabeth bleeds, she must feel that her body is failing her. She must wonder what she has done wrong. I imagine Elizabeth railing at God. She begs, cajoles, cries, screams. And nothing happens. She grows old and gives up hope. She spends her life longing, a shell of a human being. And she has no idea that God has a plan.

Can we ever know what God has in store for us? Is there ever a way, with our limited capacity, to understand the unfolding of the story? We cannot see who we will become. We cannot see how we will be formed and shaped by the struggles of our lives. Elizabeth becomes a joyful, mature, wise mother—perhaps in part because of the wisdom of age and the fulfillment of her deep longing. She has a child only when she lets go of the possibility. She understands in a profound way that her son is a gift from God. He is not hers, not even from the beginning. He has always belonged to God.

We must hold our lives with the same understanding, the same gratitude that Elizabeth finally has when she welcomes her son. He comes to her when she accepts that it is not her right to have him at all. Our lives are not our own. They belong to God and God alone. We are hosts, recipients of the gift of life.

Just by being born, you have won the lottery. You have no innate right to be here. God has created you out of love. Your life is a gift. How does this understanding impact how you live?

First Thursday of Advent
To Be Afraid

When Zechariah saw him, he was terrified; and fear overwhelmed him.

Luke 1:12

Zechariah and Elizabeth have prayed all their lives. All their lives! And yet, when the angel appears, Zechariah is troubled. The ancient Greek word used in the passage means to move back and forth, to be restless or agitated. In other words, Zechariah is used to praying, but when it comes to hearing an answer, he is unprepared. The angel literally makes him shake in his boots.

Who really wants to hear from God? To hear from God means to interact with the One who exists beyond time and space, the One who truly knows what is best for us, the One who is willing to sacrifice his son for us. That One is quite intimidating. If we are truly honest, many of us would rather talk to God than actually hear from God. God might make us change, and that idea can make us shake in our boots.

Often when I pray, I feel as if I am a running up to touch something incredibly beautiful and mysterious, a tangible assurance that God is there. I am like a child reaching for a parent's hand or calling out in the dark, straining to hear a parent's familiar voice. I want to know God is there and that God loves me, then I want to go about running my own life by myself. I don't want God to lead me, I just want God to comfort me along the way…my way.

We want God to reassure us, to give us peace. We don't want suffering, discomfort, demands, or discord. But it is likely that God may ask us to endure any or all of these things. After all, God asks a lot of Jesus. No wonder we are afraid.

Zechariah knows enough to realize that his entire life is about to change. He knows enough to be afraid. His fear is a sign of his devotion. By fearing God, he is acknowledging that much will be asked of him. He is acknowledging that a true angel stands before him, an agent of God's will, a messenger from the Holy.

Fear in and of itself is not a bad thing. It is our response to fear that defines us. Do we run and hide? Do we, like Jonah, try to run as far away from God as we can? Or do we stand in fear and listen for God's will? To be afraid is to be human. To be afraid is to recognize our limitations. We must learn to live with fear and not run from it if we are to follow Christ.

What scares you? How can you learn to live with your fears instead of running from them?

First Friday of Advent
Getting What We Want

But the angel said to him, "Do not be afraid, Zechariah,
for your prayer has been heard. Your wife Elizabeth
will bear you a son, and you will name him John. You
will have joy and gladness, and many will rejoice at his
birth, for he will be great in the sight of the Lord.

Luke 1:13-15

Zechariah is about to get exactly what he wants. He wants
a son more than anything in the world. And to hear that
his son is to be great before the Lord…what more could he
want? This is everything he has dreamed of—and more.

And his first response is doubt. Zechariah asks, "How can
this be true? I am an old man and my wife is old…"

Good news is hard to hear. It is easier to despair, to worry,
to remain unsatisfied. Sometimes I think that we humans
just can't believe that we are worthy of God's love. Bad
news, self-hatred, fear…they are easier to swallow. How

can we believe that God might want to give us everything that we ask for? What does it take to believe in the goodness of God?

Zechariah has given up hope. He is convinced that he will die without an heir. He is old, and his dreams and bloodline are nearing the end. He is resigned to his childless fate.

How many of us resign ourselves to what we consider to be our fate? *I have a weight problem...I am just not very smart...I can't cook...I can't be married...I will never find happiness.* Despair breeds despair. The more we believe in our failures, the larger they become. Like a noose around the neck, they begin to strangle us until our vision is clouded and the world looks very dark indeed.

The angel silences Zechariah not because Zechariah is a bad man but because he has succumbed to despair. He needs to open his eyes to see the goodness of God. Often this happens best when we stop talking and open our hearts. The goodness of God is all around us, but we must be willing to look. We must be willing to listen.

This old man, so used to talking and hearing the sound of his own voice, is suddenly silenced. And in his silence, he becomes like a child again, forced to listen, forced to approach life differently. Zechariah is shut up so that his heart can open up.

Do you trust in God? Do you trust in the One who performs miracles? Are you able to conceive of a reality in which God's will is for the reconciliation of all humanity?

Do you believe this is possible or do you listen to and repeat the voices of despair that so readily take up space in your mind?

Do you need to stop talking and start listening? Do you sometimes despair about your life and/or the state of the world? Can you sit back and listen to God's voice of love? Can you hear the good news?

First Saturday of Advent
Silenced by God

But now, because you did not believe my words, which will be fulfilled in their time, you will become mute, unable to speak, until the day these things occur.
Luke 1:20

As a priest myself, I readily admit that we preachers can be full of hot air. We are so used to talking that sometimes we forget how to listen. You should hear us when we gather at a conference together and worship. We are so loud. Everyone is used to hearing the sound of his or her own voice above all others.

Zechariah likes to talk. When the angel appears and gives him the news that his wife will bear a child, he immediately starts talking. How can he have a son at his age, much less Elizabeth's? How is this physically possible?

Mary asks a similar question when the angel appears to her. She asks how she will get pregnant when she is still a virgin. So why does God silence Zechariah and take away his voice for nine months while Mary gets to keep on talking?

I think the answer is simple. Zechariah needs to learn how to listen. He needs to stop giving all the answers and try to simply pay attention. *Keep your mouth shut and let me be God*, says the angel. *You talk too much.*

A hundred years ago, worship lasted much longer than the sixty-minute-services we're used to today. Sermons were longer too. Why? In the days before TV and computers and instant communication, men and women toiled in fields and kitchens. Silence was a constant companion. When they came to worship, they were hungry for words.

Now we are starved for silence. Our ears are bombarded by sound and our minds by constant streams of information. We are not starved for words; we are starved for silence.

The angel knows that Zechariah needs to get ready to be a father. And in order to prepare, he needs to stop talking. He needs to listen.

We too should listen to the voice of the angel. Stop the talking, the angel says. If you want to get ready for the birth of Christ, you must learn to embrace the silence. Stop the constant stream of words. Turn off the flow of information. Sit in the silence of not knowing, not answering, not resolving, not responding. Let the mess be a mess. Just be.

Today we can't hear God because of the roar inside our own minds. We must cultivate silence as if it is in danger of becoming extinct. We must plant it, nurture it, harvest it.

I have taken to embracing silence in worship, pausing before we pray. After my sermon, I make myself sit in silence with the entire congregation for one minute. This sounds like a short amount of time, but it can feel like an eternity when you are waiting for God to speak.

A few years ago, I conducted a funeral. A parishioner shared with me an exchange she overheard from a visiting couple. The man leaned over to his wife: "I like that Moorehead lady, but she seems to lose her place a lot." The man could not conceive of intentional silence in worship so he assumed I had gotten lost or forgotten my words.

Maybe God is asking us to lose our place from time to time, to stop the talking and be lost for a bit. It might give God the chance to show us the way.

Do you carve out moments of silence in your day? If not, could you find a way to do so?

Second Sunday of Advent
John

John the baptizer appeared in the wilderness,
proclaiming a baptism of repentance for the
forgiveness of sins.

Mark 1:4

John grows up the son of a high priest of the temple. His mother is descended from the line of Aaron. He surely has the very best education the Levites can afford. He is well-versed in scripture and in the richness of the Jewish tradition. He has access to the best of everything in Jerusalem.

When does John determine that God wants him to leave his privileged life and set out for the wilderness? Is it after the death of his parents? Does grief propel him out of the civilized social strata and into the desert? What is it like to leave such a structured, privileged life and enter into a life of dirt and survival? From books and lectures to total solitude. From fine clothes and robes to rags and camels' hair. And locusts. Seriously. Does John welcome the change?

Does he feel like this is what God is asking him to do? To leave his old life and enter into a new one?

I imagine John is a restless man. Determined to serve God, he may feel suffocated by the trappings of the temple, the hierarchy, and rules. Perhaps John leaves for the desert in order to find silence, in order to listen. We will never know for sure.

There are many gaps in the story. Just as with Jesus, we hear of John's birth and then we see him as a fully developed prophet. There is no mention of his growth, his struggles, his liminal period. The extraordinary child simply transforms into an extraordinary man. This must be enough.

As the mother of teenagers, I wish we could have more of the details of John's adolescence. I wish we could see the differentiation, when John chose to leave. Was it painful for John? Was it painful for his parents? Was there yelling and slamming of doors? Guilt trips? Tears?

In order for each of us to reach our potential as human beings, we must leave home and risk change. We must leave the comfort of childhood in order to truly discern God's will. John has the strength to leave everything that he knows behind. He has the courage to risk becoming himself.

Do you have the courage to seek God first? Are you willing to leave your comfort zone to become who God created you to be?

Second Monday of Advent
Making a Straight Path

The voice of one crying out in the wilderness: "Prepare the way of the Lord, make his paths straight."

Mark 1:3

Francisco "Cisco" Anglero was born in Puerto Rico in 1944. His family moved to Brooklyn in 1949. Cisco was dark skinned and couldn't speak English well so he was frequently beaten up when he went out into the neighborhood. By the time he was big enough to fight back, he was so full of rage that he beat his bullies with a baseball bat. He took up body-building and became a drug dealer. His life was consumed with violence.

No matter how bad his life got, there was one place where he could find peace. Whenever he came home to the family's small apartment, Cisco's mother would be sitting in a rocking chair with the Bible in her lap. She would always smile and thank God for his safety.

When Cisco was 22, his mother died. This loss sent his life spiraling into total chaos. He was caught with drugs and thrown in jail. Two men in prison kept inviting him to a church service, but every time they asked, he refused, turned up his music up, and rolled over in bed. Still, they would not give up. Their persistence really irritated him.

One Sunday the men came by and asked again. Cisco tried to ignore them but his radio would not work. He tried to turn on the TV. It wouldn't work either. He rolled over and tried to ignore the men but suddenly he felt like he was going to crawl out of his skin. He finally relented and joined the men for church.

Cisco stood in the back while the prisoners sang. And there, up at the front, he saw his mother. She was looking right at him, singing and smiling. When they asked people to come forward, she waved him up. He saw the path, the aisle between the metal folding chairs. It was wide open.

Cisco walked toward his mother and received the bread and wine. Leaving the altar, he looked back; his mother was nowhere to be seen. Cisco knew right away that his life had changed forever. His love for his mother—and her love for him—had made a path to God.

Make his paths straight. That's what John says. And I never knew what John meant until I read about this story. John is asking us to clear a path to God. As if we were shoveling snow in winter, we should work to clear away the clutter of our lives, the distractions, the broken relationships. Clear the path, make way for Christ.

When Cisco's life was nothing but violence and chaos, he saw a path from the front door of his apartment to his mother's rocking chair. Her love made a way forward for him. Cisco eventually worked his way out of prison and became a mentor for troubled youth. His mother, the one person who truly loved him, made a straight path for him to find God. When God called Cisco, God simply showed him the path to his mother.

How can you make a path straight to God? How can you love in such a transformational way that you create a way for people to come to know God?

Second Tuesday of Advent
Looking Outward

I am not worthy to untie the thong of his sandal.
John 1:27

With his education and charism, John is a formidable
figure. He draws crowds, inspiring people to walk great
distances from cities and towns and into the desert to hear
him. He must be an incredible speaker and preacher—
Jesus will later refer to John the Baptist as the greatest of
the prophets.

Yet John never boasts of his own deeds. He never seeks
the center of attention. When people try to follow him, he
points them to Jesus.

John is not interested in himself. He does not denigrate
or talk negatively about himself. He just does not seem to
find himself very interesting. His entire focus is on waiting
for Jesus—and when Jesus comes, his focus stays on Jesus.

In the early part of the twentieth century, the Christian mystic Evelyn Underhill wrote in her book, *The Ways of the Spirit*, "Don't let us waste much time gazing at ourselves. A deepened and enriched sense of God is far more important than increased and detailed knowledge of self."

American culture is built upon the cult of the self. From childhood, we are focused on the self. The jobs we pursue often are related to how well they will pay us. Giving and serving are practiced but only if they will enhance the self. Even preachers promote what is often called the "Prosperity Gospel," where good service to God will translate into the self becoming happy and prosperous. The first priority is the self.

Another kind of self-absorption practiced in this country is hatred of self. Still a focus on the self, this type of behavior is obsessed with self-criticism and self-hatred. This dark and devious self-idolatry leads to deep insecurities, alcoholism, mental and physical disorders, and other issues.

John does not focus on himself. He focuses on the One whose sandal he is not worthy to untie. Focusing on God leads to freedom. Focusing on God leads to peace. The self will be at peace when it is no longer the center of the universe. Only God is large enough to take center stage.

Have you become absorbed with yourself? How can you turn your attention back to God?

Second Wednesday of Advent
The Humble Ask Questions

Are you the one who is to come, or are we to wait for another?

Matthew 11:3

If John has a message to preach, why would he have to move away from people? Why not stay and spread the news of repentance right there in Jerusalem? John must believe that listening is more important than preaching. And he knows that he can hear better in the desert, away from the crowds and cacophony.

It is scary to listen to God. You must be willing to silence the noise around you. You must be willing to make space in your mind. Have you ever cleaned up a very messy room? You have to lift clothes off the floor, take laundry baskets downstairs, take out the trash. It is a lot of effort to make space, to clean things up, to make a path straight.

When you pray, if you chose to really listen, it is a forceful act. Your thoughts will rush at you like an oncoming train, and you must constantly put them aside. *Yes, I hear you. Wait. Let me clear a space in my mind for God. Let me clear a path.*

John has the courage to listen. Really listen.

No one is more revered by Jesus, more honored, than John the Baptist. "Of those born of women, there is no one greater," Jesus says.

At the end of his life, John is still listening. The voices of darkness and doubt enter his mind when he is in prison. He wonders if he has made a mistake. Maybe his entire life has been in vain. Maybe Jesus is not the Messiah after all.

Just before his death, John sends a message to Jesus: "Are you the one who is to come, or are we to wait for another?"

Did I make a mistake? Was this all a big mistake?

John doubts at the end. He wonders if he listened to the right words. And this, more than any other part of John's life, makes me admire him. John listens so hard, with so much passion and fervor, that he is even willing to admit that he might be wrong. He is willing to consider that he might have staked his whole life on the wrong man.

The thing that scares me the most about religious extremists is the certainty with which they act. Not only do extremists believe that God asks them to kill, but they seem to be so certain in the instructions. Holy men, like John the Baptist, have room to doubt. Holy men and women are always listening, always willing to admit that they might be wrong. They are people who live the questions.

Are you certain of your religious views? Of your political views? Are you willing to ask questions? Are you willing to learn from others?

Second Thursday of Advent
Killing the Critic

*[Herod] sent and had John beheaded in the prison.
The head was brought on a platter and given to the
girl, who brought it to her mother.*

Matthew 14:10-11

King Herod Agrippa is married to Herodias, the wife
of his brother Phillip. I cannot imagine what family
dinners must have been like. Talk about a soap opera!
Taking your brother's wife while he is still alive is a pretty
awful example of sibling rivalry. It is cruel and selfish,
but Herod is king, and like David before him, he takes
what he wants, whether it's right or not. Herodias seems
to be flattered with her elevation to queen. But deep
down, they both know they are wrong. Yet no one dares
challenge them.

Most of the public have either forgotten that Herod
has taken his brother's wife or they are too scared to
say anything, but then John the Baptist comes along.

John speaks out against Herod's actions, saying "it was unlawful for you to have" the brother's wife.

Angry at John's insolence, Herod throws John in prison. He does not execute him right away because the crowd regards John as a prophet, and Herod doesn't want to raise their ire. While John is prison, Herod calls upon John and listens to him with fascination. I doubt Herod has ever met anyone quite like John before. John both fascinates and perplexes Herod. But Herod's wife hates John because he criticized her in public.

Considering John's truth a personal affront, Herodias wants him dead. The most deeply insecure people do not just hate those who point out their flaws; they want to kill them. Herodias uses her own daughter to carry out the evil plan. The younger Herodias dances for her stepfather on his birthday, and the performance pleases him so much that he promises to grant her whatever she might wish. Her mother perhaps whispers in her daughter's ear: *Ask for the head of John the Baptist.*

I can only imagine the look on King Herod's face when his own daughter publicly asks for the beheading of John the Baptist, whom many consider a holy man. Herod has a choice between his reputation and the life of an innocent man. All his friends are looking at him as he weighs his options. Herod chooses his reputation. Just like Pontius Pilate, Herod is willing to murder an innocent man rather than look bad in front of his royal subjects. He is willing to kill rather than be shamed or mocked. He would rather murder than admit to a mistake.

For most of us, the choice is not so stark but we still face the same dilemma. How much do you care about what people think of you? Are you willing to lie to preserve your reputation? What are you willing to sacrifice for your good name?

Second Friday of Advent
The Mixed Emotions of Mary

And [the angel] came to her and said, "Greetings, favored one! The Lord is with you." But she was much perplexed by his words and pondered what sort of greeting this might be.

Luke 1:28-29

When the angel comes to Mary, scripture tells us that she goes through a variety of emotions. She is greatly troubled. Wouldn't you be? Mary is upset by the angel. This is not what she expected. This is not according to her plan. Scripture is clear that she is troubled by what the angel is telling her, that God is with her. Mary seems to instinctively know that her life is going to change forever. And she is not sure what she wants.

Mary does not ask the angel who he is. She does not seem afraid of the angel but rather is perplexed by his message. I wonder: Has she seen an angel before? She does not seem frightened by his appearance (most people are blinded or terribly frightened by angels). Rather she is troubled because she knows that something tremendous will be asked of her. Luke writes that she "tried to discern what sort of greeting this might be." She is troubled that the angel called her favored one.

We depict Mary as a placid, perhaps timid, young woman. Calm. Pretty. Virtuous. In paintings and poems and stories, Mary is never disheveled, nervous, or unsure. Just pure peace and tranquility. But this is not how her character is depicted in the original Greek. I wonder why the English translations play down her emotions, why our stories tell of a tepid Mary, not a feisty one. The original text reveals Mary as a young woman full of expression and emotion.

When God enters our hearts, I suspect our emotions are more similar to Mary's as described in the Greek text. We feel many different emotions, including being troubled and confused.

Mary was complicated. The one chosen to bear God's son felt many different emotions. How does that make you feel?

Second Saturday of Advent
The Right Kind of Question

Mary said to the angel, "How can this be, since I am a virgin?"

Luke 1:34

When an angel comes to Zechariah, he asks the angel a question and is silenced for nine months. When the angel comes to Mary and she asks a question, the angel seems to think it is fine, and she continues to speak.

Why is one question punished and the other accepted? Both ask how the birth of their children will be possible. Zechariah asks because he is old. Mary asks because she is young and inexperienced. Why is Zechariah silenced? Are there good questions and bad questions when it comes to our relationship with God? I believe that all questions are good. My working theory is that Zechariah is questioning God's ability whereas Mary is questioning the method by which the event will take place.

Regardless of the reasoning, we can never fully comprehend the relationship between God and anyone but ourselves. We cannot know where other human beings stand with God, if they are saved or not, if they have displeased God or given God great pleasure. We cannot know the salvation of others because God alone determines this most intimate relationship. It is our place to manifest the love of God but not the judgment of God. God alone can judge.

What would the world look like if all human beings could agree that it is God's job to determine salvation and not our purview? We could hear the stories of other faiths and share our stories. We could dance together and share our knowledge without fear. We could let God be God. Wouldn't that be beautiful?

Have you attempted to determine the salvation of others or to judge the nature of their relationship with God? Do you think that you have that ability or right? Why or why not?

Third Sunday of Advent
The Questions Not Answered

The angel said to her, "The Holy Spirit will come upon you, and the power of the Most High will overshadow you; therefore the child to be born will be holy; he will be called Son of God."

Luke 1:35

When Mary asks how the pregnancy will happen, the angel gives her a rather vague answer. There are no concrete details at all. She is not told how she will survive, since unwed mothers are sometimes stoned to death. She is not told how she will eat, where she will live, who will care for her. She is told that the Holy Spirit will overshadow her and that the child will be great. He will be the Son of God. Sure, it sounds good, but what exactly does "overshadow" mean? Give this woman some details!

Mary must have many unanswered questions. But she does not ask any more. She just agrees. She says, "Here am I, the servant of the Lord; let it be with me according to your word." In other words, Mary says, *Thy will be done.*

Mary has no insurance policy, no hold-harmless clause or backup plan. She has no definitive path forward. She has no idea what tomorrow will bring, and yet she professes to do what God asks because she is God's servant.

This is the ultimate challenge for all of us. When God calls on us, how will we respond? How many details will we require before we make a decision? Who is in charge?

We will certainly not be able to bring Christ into the world until we set this matter straight. The choice is up to us: We can serve the self, or we can serve God, but we cannot serve both.

I cannot tell you how many times people have come to my office to tell me that they want to pray or they want to serve, but on their own schedule, the fourth Fridays or on rainy Sundays with no bowl games or opportunity to golf. We cannot radically alter the world if we are only willing to serve God on the side or if we wait until we have all the answers before agreeing to follow Christ. If we are to bring Christ into the world, we must put our own needs aside and be willing to be inconvenienced, even changed.

We have one holy and precious life. Who will you serve?

Third Monday of Advent
Support System

And now, your relative Elizabeth in her old age has also conceived a son; and this is the sixth month for her who was said to be barren. For nothing will be impossible with God.

Luke 1:36-37

The angel does not give Mary a lot of details about how this pregnancy will work or how she will survive, but the angel does give her a friend. The angel tells her that her cousin is pregnant, too. Perhaps this is the most comforting information the angel offers Mary.

When I was pregnant, I was eager to be around relatives. I also looked forward to being around other pregnant women, to hear about their experiences. When the angel tells Mary about Elizabeth, the angel is giving Mary a support system.

When people come to the church, they want information about what we believe and how they can join and who is in charge. Often all this information is not nearly as important as the answer to one simple question: *Who will love me?* Those who come to the faith alone and try to set out on that journey without deep and abiding support often wander away. Those who have a friend, a mentor, a sponsor, or small group move deeper into the faith.

Alcoholics Anonymous mandates that each person have a sponsor. The organization knows from experience that lasting change needs outside support. Every one of us needs someone to call, to ask, to lean on. Mary needs Elizabeth more than she needs answers to her questions. God makes sure that she is not alone. She has a woman friend to guide her.

I cannot stress enough the importance of companionship along the spiritual journey. This is more important than books or knowledge or creeds. Walking with someone, praying with someone, being truly honest with someone enables us to follow Christ. None of us can do this alone.

Do you have a spiritual companion? Do you have a support system? Do you pray with others about what is going on in your life?

Third Tuesday of Advent
Changing Everything

In those days Mary arose and went with haste to the hill country, to a town in Judah, and she entered the house of Zechariah and greeted Elizabeth.

Luke 1:39-40

Zechariah and Elizabeth must have moved when he became mute and she became pregnant. They are living in the hill country in a town in Judah when Mary comes to visit. I suppose Zechariah can no longer serve as a high priest without a voice.

Oh, how their lives have changed. The once confident, eloquent Zechariah is now silent. The only voice in the house is of his elderly pregnant wife. Does Elizabeth dare ask him to bring her a glass of water in an era when women waited on men? Was the house suddenly silent? Did they no longer feel comfortable in the hustle and bustle of Jerusalem? Did the high society life of a Levite seem empty?

Hearing from God in a big way often rattles the cage. Everything in our lives shifts. Things that once comforted us no longer seem appropriate. Behaviors that we used to think were normal no longer seem healthy. Our houses feel uncomfortable; our lives don't fit.

The angel began a process when he spoke to Zechariah. This was about a new chapter in the life of an old man and his wife. All of a sudden, everything was different.

Sometimes I think that hearing from God must be like falling in love. It turns everything upside down. You realize that you were asleep before, and now you are awake. And the world looks different.

Is there a point in your life when God woke you up?

Third Wednesday of Advent
Overwhelmed by Beauty

When Elizabeth heard Mary's greeting, the child leaped in her womb. And Elizabeth was filled with the Holy Spirit.

Luke 1:41

Mary comes to visit her cousin for companionship but also for shelter. She is safer away from Nazareth. When the people of Nazareth see her belly grow, they might punish her, even stone her to death for being pregnant out of wedlock. Mary needs a place where she is safe.

It takes Mary a long time to walk to Judea from Nazareth. It is some ninety miles of rough terrain, and Mary is pregnant, her ankles surely swollen, her back aching. Is she traveling alone or does she walk with others? Luke does not tell us. She must be frightened to travel so far in the heat with a child growing in her womb.

When Mary walks through the door of her cousin's house, the baby inside Elizabeth leaps. Little John is doing a dance in his momma's belly! And Elizabeth is thrilled. She begins to prophesy. "Blessed are you among women, and blessed is the fruit of your womb."

Elizabeth is overwhelmed with what God is doing. She sings of Mary's favor with God.

Throughout the ages, there are stories of saints going into a kind of ecstasy: They see something so beautiful, so clearly of God, that they begin to weep or sing or write. Saint Francis of Assisi is said to have had tears stream down his face when he experienced something extraordinary in nature. I imagine this is how Elizabeth is responding. She is simply overwhelmed by what God is doing.

The connection between pregnant women is a divine mystery. I remember the feeling when I was pregnant—so much joy, so much to share. No doubt Elizabeth is lonely and has longed for a companion. She has spent the first six months of her pregnancy virtually in hiding and with a mute husband to boot! She is ready for a friend. But more than that, Elizabeth is a woman of prayer who can see something incredible is happening.

When have you been overwhelmed by the beauty of creation or the miracles of God? Have you longed to share it with others? Have you been able to do so?

Third Thursday of Advent
The Song

And Mary said, "My soul magnifies the Lord, and my spirit rejoices in God my Savior."

Luke 1:46-47

One of my first memories is of lying underneath my mother's piano and listening as the music poured over me in waves. Bach, Beethoven, Mozart—I had no names for the composers, no words to articulate the intricate beauty of the notes strung together to create such beauty. But I heard it. I absorbed the music, and it shaped my heart and soul.

Luke must be either a musician or a poet. In writing his gospel, Luke includes four great canticles. These songs are all reminiscent of the hymns of praise in Israel's psalter. He begins with pure praise to God, and all four songs flow out of that same ecstasy. This event, the birth of the Son of God, is too much for mere words. It can only be expressed through music.

Zechariah sings when his voice returns. Mary sings when she meets her cousin Elizabeth. The angels sing to announce the birth to the shepherds, and the old man Simeon sings when he sees the Christ child. These songs have become the bedrock of daily worship in liturgical churches across the world, from Roman Catholic to Anglican to Eastern Orthodox. These songs of praise are the first Christian worship.

Sometimes when I pray alone, I don't know how to express my love for God so I begin to sing. Speaking in tongues can also sound like a kind of singing. There are moments when words fail us; we are caught in the limits of language, and the spoken word is no longer adequate to reflect the glory of God. We become overwhelmed, and music is the least inadequate form of expression.

Mary sings a song. She sings to her baby. She sings to her cousin. She sings to God. Her song is a way of saying thank you for something too great for mere words.

I have heard it said that music is the universal language. Perhaps in heaven, all communication is done through music. I would not mind that at all.

How do you express your love of God? What is your favorite kind of music?

Third Friday of Advent
The Power of Mary

Surely, from now on all generations will call me blessed.
Luke 1:48

I learned a poem as a child:

> Mary, Mary, meek and mild.
> Jesus Christ, her little child.

I used to picture Mary this way, as meek, mild, passive, gentle, weak. But then I really read the *Magnificat*, her song of praise. And I realized she was none of these things.

In this glorious song, Mary makes a powerful cosmic claim about the child she carries. She speaks of holiness, of power, of casting down the mighty from their thrones. She speaks kingly language. She speaks of a man who will change the world.

But Mary does not just praise the child. She also claims her role in this event. She owns the fact that for generations to come, people will call her blessed. *The Almighty has done great things for me*, she says.

Mary is not shy to sing about herself. She is not some wallflower trying to blend into her surroundings. She sings God's praises and claims her divine right to have a place in the gospel story. She is a woman of power and presence. This is not meek and mild.

The word *Magnificat* has the same root as the verb to magnify. Mary is claiming that her soul is magnifying God. She uses herself to shine God's light into the world. Her role is vital, and she asserts her place in the salvation story.

Are we as believers supposed to be humble and quiet, self-effacing and demure? Is that really true? What does it mean to be humble? Mary sees that her role has been given to her by God and that without God, she will be nothing. But with God, she understands that she is something else. With God, she is a powerful woman who will change the course of history.

There is an incredible statue of Mary in Butte, Montana. Mary stands over sixty feet high. Her arms are outstretched as if to embrace the world. She is powerful, radiant, protective. Surely the one who bore the Son of God must have been all of these things. Surely she must have been something else.

Does God want us to be confident? How should we embrace our gifts with gratitude and holy humility?

Third Saturday of Advent
Reversal of Power

He has brought down the powerful from their thrones, and lifted up the lowly.

Luke 1:52

In her song of praise, Mary tells about a reversal of power. She sings of the strong becoming weak and the weak becoming strong. She talks about scattering the proud, feeding the hungry, and leaving the rich empty and alone. She proclaims God who remembers a promise.

The Hebrew people envision a world of fairness, of equality, of justice. They believe that when God takes over running the world, things will come back into order, and the inequalities will work themselves out. We will move back into harmony with God and with one another.

Mary is singing of the Hebrew faith. She is retelling the story of God and what God has already done. She proclaims how God is fulfilling a promise to the Hebrew people. Somehow, Mary knows that the birth of this child will be another revelation of the very same promise that God made with the people of Israel in the desert. This is part of God's response, God's plan to live out a promise.

Often, when we pray, we assume God will answer in a human way. We assume God will respond quickly and with one answer, just as a person would answer a question or do a task for another person. But God is divine, and God's answers are multi-dimensional. God's responses don't always come at once, in some clear linear progression, and there may be more than one answer to just one question. Sometimes, God answers a question with a question. (I find that particularly frustrating!)

Even at her tender age, Mary understands that this child is an answer to the prayers of the Hebrew people. This is God's response to the people of Israel, and it is far beyond her understanding. Mary is open to the possibility that God might answer in a way she might not fully comprehend.

We often fail to notice or acknowledge God's answers because they are too advanced for our limited consciousness. If you have made a request of God and you don't think that God has answered, look more deeply. Open your eyes and ears in the present moment in which you are living and breathing. Truly listen. Be awake. Most of the time it is not God who neglects to answer, but it is we who neglect to listen.

Do you know how to truly listen for God's response to your prayers?

Fourth Sunday of Advent
The Shame of Joseph

Her husband Joseph, being a righteous man and unwilling to expose her to public disgrace, planned to dismiss her quietly. **Matthew 1:19**

Joseph is a carpenter by trade. He has studied and apprenticed under another carpenter, perhaps his father. It has taken Joseph years to establish his own practice, to gain the confidence of the people of Nazareth. He is older than Mary, secure enough in his business to take on a wife and perhaps eventually provide for a family.

Joseph has surely seen Mary in the village but he probably has not spoken to her. A man does not speak to a woman who is not his wife or relative. But he might have watched her talk with other girls or go to the well for water. At some point, he has decided she could be a good wife.

How does Joseph find out that Mary is pregnant? Does her father tell him? Does he hear it in the village? Does she have a slight baby bump? Imagine Joseph's humiliation. Put yourself in his position. This is the woman he has chosen, and someone has violated her. Someone has ruined her. In this time period, a woman is not considered a person in her own right but rather a vessel for the purpose of bearing children. The word for woman in the New Testament Greek literally means *walking womb*. She is a vessel for the purpose of having children—preferably boys. Mary is Joseph's property! He has reserved her. She is betrothed. This pregnancy is the ultimate insult to Joseph's manhood, all his careful plans ruined. He must feel such shame.

Joseph is a gentle man. He does not rage (or not that scripture recounts). I think Joseph must love Mary even before they were to be married, for when he discovers she is pregnant, he wants to "dismiss her quietly." This would be a tremendous, selfless gift. Many women pregnant outside of wedlock were stoned to death. Perhaps by not publicly shunning her, Joseph will save her life.

Do people make fun of him? Feel sorry for him? Surely his friends tell him to move on, to pick another woman, a virgin. Who wants a woman who is unfaithful? In a village the size of Nazareth, where everyone knew everyone, the gossip must be intense and swift. Joseph and his pregnant fiancée are the scandal of the day. The ruin of a young woman. The shame of a young man.

Joseph was shamed along the path to bringing Christ into the world. Have you felt shame? Have you ever shamed others?

Fourth Monday of Advent
Son of David

*But just when he had resolved to do this, an angel
of the Lord appeared to him in a dream and said,
"Joseph, son of David, do not be afraid to take Mary
as your wife, for the child conceived in her is from the
Holy Spirit. She will bear a son, and you are to name
him Jesus, for he will save his people from their sins."*
Matthew 1:20-21

The angel addresses Joseph as Son of David. The angel
appeals to Joseph's higher nature, to his genealogy and
reminds Joseph that he is the descendant of a king and
that from his offspring, the Messiah is to come.

Joseph—not Mary—is the descendant of David. Jesus will
become his son by adoption. Joseph fulfills his destiny as
a descendant of David by conquering his fear, subduing
his shame, and taking as a wife a pregnant woman. David
commits a sin with Bathsheba, impregnating her while she
is married to another man and then having her husband

killed so he can have her for his own. His descendant Joseph embodies the antithesis of this selfish behavior, willing to trust in God and protect and marry a pregnant woman.

What is heroism? The people of Israel believe that a descendant of David will lead them in battle against Rome and liberate them from oppression. Joseph does none of these things. But his actions change the world. A simple act of kindness. A simple act of trust. Joseph opens his home. He opens his heart. The greatest kind of heroism is sometimes the courage to love in the face of despair.

Joseph shames himself when he takes in Mary. He is laughed at, scorned as a man with no spine.

Heroism is found in the person willing to do what is right, who lets go of the opinions of others and trusts in God alone.

Are you willing to sacrifice the opinions of others in order to please God? Is your relationship with God your most important relationship?

Fourth Tuesday of Advent
Time to Think

When Joseph awoke from sleep, he did as the angel of the Lord commanded him; he took her as his wife, but had no marital relations with her until she had borne a son; and he named him Jesus.

Matthew 1:24-25

The Gospel of Matthew describes Joseph as a just man. When Joseph learns Mary is pregnant, he does not act rashly or impulsively. He considers. He thinks. He doesn't let his disappointment or shame overcome his rational mind. He takes time. And thank God for that. If Joseph had acted like many of us would—on impulse—he would have done something before he went to sleep, before God has the chance to speak to him in a dream.

I am convinced that hastiness is akin to darkness when it comes to making important decisions. When in doubt, wait and pray. Acting on pure emotion can often be a mistake when it comes to life-altering decisions. Elegant solutions and compromises usually develop and unfold over time. Joseph seems to understand this when he takes time to *consider these things*.

God takes millennia to form mountains and nine months to shape a child in its mother's womb. Most of what God does takes time. There is a reason why church seasons like Advent and even Christmas are not just one day. If we are to follow God's will, we must be willing to wait, pray, and consider these things—just like Joseph.

Have you made a rash decision and lived to regret it? Do you have any decisions coming up that you can ponder and consider like Joseph does?

Fourth Wednesday of Advent
God in a Census

Joseph also went from the town of Nazareth in Galilee to Judea, to the city of David called Bethlehem, because he was descended from the house and family of David. He went to be registered with Mary, to whom he was engaged and who was expecting a child.
Luke 2:4-5

Joseph is told to take his wife and travel to Bethlehem to be counted. He is forced to leave his home, his carpentry business, and his family and friends. It seems so unfair: The purpose of the census is to be counted for taxation purposes. Essentially, Joseph has to uproot his life so that the government can collect taxes.

And yet, the journey that Joseph and Mary are forced to take enables the Christ child to fulfill the ancient prophecy about the place that the Messiah was to be born—in Bethlehem, in the land of Judah, where David was raised. Rome oppresses its people and forces mass migration to the place of peoples' birth, but God is able to use even the most unjust structures to fulfill a prophecy.

Is it possible that God might be able to act even through the government—even through things as oppressive and boring as taxes? Can God work through the IRS? Maybe that is taking it too far!

But seriously, isn't God, the Almighty One, able to take even the most oppressive of structures and use them for higher purposes? Is not God able to work even within the confines of the broken powers and unjust structures of our own day?

No matter what happens to you in life, I think we as Christians can ask ourselves: Where is God in this? How can I find grace in even the worst of circumstances?

How can you see God's hand at work even when you have to follow instructions that you don't want to follow?

Fourth Thursday of Advent
A Quiet Man

He went to be registered with Mary, to whom he was engaged and who was expecting a child. While they were there, the time came for her to deliver her child.
Luke 2:5-6

Joseph never speaks in the gospel accounts. He does not ask questions as Mary or Zechariah do when the angel appears to them. He accepts the meaning of his dream. He moves when God asks him to move. He weds Mary without further questions.

This quiet obedience makes Joseph remarkable. Most of us would have complained a bit. I know I would! I would have asked why. I would have resented moving. I would have been furious about having to relocate to another country with a toddler in tow! But Joseph is just quiet.

He reminds me of the man who fixes our garbage disposal. He smiles, listens to our urgent requests, and then proceeds to fix it. Joseph speaks through his actions and not with his words.

We live in a verbose age. Words blanket us every day, from emails to texts to TV and radio. We are enveloped in language, and it slides over us like water, like the air we breathe. We swim in words. We breathe them. We throw words around as if they are disposable and can be taken back or discarded. Words have become cheap.

I don't often remember what folks say. What I remember is what they do. Do they give away money to help the world? Do they hold open a door? Do they visit the sick and suffering?

Much can be communicated without words. Silence in this day and age is powerful. It speaks volumes. Many of us are afraid of its wisdom, afraid of what we might hear when all the words cease and the eloquence of God is expressed in silence.

The man who raises the Son of God as his own child does so without uttering a word in scripture. What might his silence be saying to us?

How can you expand the silence in your life? How can you speak less and listen more?

Fourth Friday of Advent

And she gave birth to her firstborn son and wrapped him in bands of cloth, and laid him in a manger, because there was no place for them in the inn.

Luke 2:7

Bethlehem is crowded because of Herod's orders that everyone return to the place of their birth. Mary is going into labor, and no one has room for guests. Where can she lie down? Where will she have the baby?

The word inn is misleading. There are no Days Inns or Best Westerns in Bethlehem at the time of Jesus' birth, just houses where the homeowners might have a room or two for rent. The Greek word for inn—*kataluma*—means guest room, a place for guests. There are no innkeepers per se, no hotel managers or neon signs that indicate whether there's a vacancy. I imagine Joseph and Mary knock on the doors of several homes, only to be told each time that there is no room.

I wonder if the innkeepers of Christmas pageants have been unfairly maligned. I imagine that the people who close the doors and leave the poor young couple outside must feel horrified. It is a great honor for a Jewish family to welcome guests. But what can they do if all the rooms are taken?

Then a door opens. Someone doesn't just say no; someone says, "Wait, let me think…I do have a place where the animals stay warm…It's not very nice or comfortable, but it is all I have, and I offer it to you."

As inadequate as it is, someone offers Mary and Joseph a small cave where the animals are taking shelter from the wind. Someone at least offers that.

It is a meager act of hospitality, but God is born there. The baby Jesus is born in a place of warmth and shelter. Although it is dirty, the cave is adequate. It is enough.

God uses even the smallest of gifts, the least of ideas, the smallest of tokens, to reflect glory and love.

Sometimes even the smallest offering is enough for Christ to enter the world. What can you offer today?

Fourth Saturday of Advent
Angels

Then an angel of the Lord stood before them, and the glory of the Lord shone around them, and they were terrified.
Luke 2:9

The Bible is teeming with angels. Of course, the Christmas story features plenty of angels, but angels also play pivotal roles in many of the major events in which God acts in human history. An angel guards the gates of Eden when we are expelled. An angel flies around the Hebrews when they leave Egypt for the desert (why do we always focus on the pillars of cloud and fire and ignore the angel?) Angels appear to Abraham and Sarah to announce their pregnancy. Jacob wrestles an angel. Angels wait on Jesus in the desert and the Garden of Gethsemane, and they are present at the tomb after the resurrection.

But for all of the action by angels, we don't spend a lot of time talking about them. I wonder why. Are we worried that we might be seen as crazy or overly sentimental? Are we afraid that we will become that person who collects trinkets of fat babies with wings and chats easily about guardian angels? Do we think angels are meant only for children or the childish? Have they become the stuff of fairy tales like sprites or goblins? In other words, can you be an intellectual Christian and take angels seriously?

I believe the answer is yes! In fact, to read the scriptures and either deny or ignore the existence of angels makes no intellectual sense at all. It simply doesn't add up.

With the rise of quantum physics, even scientists will concede that there are forces far beyond human understanding. Couldn't angels be among them?

Angels are like translators for God. They come at pivotal moments when God is trying to get our complete attention. They call out to Mary and Joseph, to the shepherds, and to us. *Pay attention*, they say, and they almost always tell us to not be afraid. The angels are like bridges, carrying messages from God to us and back again, communicators of the most extraordinary kind.

Are you open to the possibility that there are angels active and engaged in this world?

Christmas Day
Birth

And the Word became flesh and lived among us.
John 1:14

Many years ago, I was attending a clergy conference when a woman said something that disturbed me. This woman, who had been preaching for about a decade, said that the gospel message was quite simple and that preaching was really just about saying the same simple message over and over again. She declared this as if it were a matter of fact and not her opinion. I was startled by her statement, but I did not comment on it. I wish I had said something.

I wish I had said that the gospel is the most beautiful, complex, mysterious, incomprehensible, life-altering, deep message that God could ever give us. It is so deep that there is no way for the human mind to ever fully conceive it. To preach about the event of the incarnation, about the Word of God becoming flesh, is to try to point to something unfathomable. It is to try and explain the existence of a mountain so large that we cannot see where it begins or ends. All we can do is describe the small portion within our sight.

Christmas is not the same old story told over and over again. Christmas is a glimpse, the chipping away at a truth that exists so far beyond human comprehension that all we can do is point to it. We must touch upon this truth over and over again for the entirety of our lives and beyond, not as repetition but as an attempt to go deeper, to approach this story from a fresh angle, to try again to plumb the depths of its meaning.

The Maker of the Universe became human flesh. The birth of Jesus is the greatest form of communication from God that we have ever known. And we will never be able to fully understand this gift that God has given us.

How can you hear this story as if it were the first time? What new revelation do you have about the birth of Christ today?

The Second Day
of Christmas
The Holy Place

And she gave birth to her firstborn son and wrapped
him in bands of cloth, and laid him in a manger.
Luke 2:7

Jesus is born in a cave. In Jesus' time, shepherds dig caves
in the side of the hills surrounding Bethlehem to shield
themselves and their livestock from the wind and rain. I
have walked these hills. No small wooden shack would
stand the test of time. When the gospels say that the baby
Jesus is laid in a manger, they mean a feeding trough used
for the livestock to eat. The gospels are not referring to
some kind of tiny wooden house that looks like it was built
by the seven dwarves and sprinkled with a little fairy dust.

Jesus is born in the dirt. In a cave.

When I was little, I used to search for the perfect hiding place, a safe space where I could put my pillows and stuffed animals. A place where the world was quiet and peaceful. In my grandmother's house, I found refuge in the back of a closet. In my own home, I played under the piano. Closets, cubbies, corners: These were all places for me to imagine another world, places where I could hear myself think.

In the movie *The War Room*, an African-American woman finds her prayer place in a closet. She places notes, pictures, and prayers on the walls. In that small space, she battles against the forces of darkness and prays for the peace of the whole world.

Quiet small spaces can be the places where we feel safe. And when we feel safe, we can open our hearts to God. Sure, God can be found in the loud frenzy of the world, in the hustle and bustle of a crowd, but when we are in a small space and alone, we can hear God. We can enter a child-like place of safety, a womb of sorts. We can birth new ideas, be inspired, find answers to our deepest questions.

The God of the Universe entered the world not in the heart of a busy town or on the altar of a holy temple but in a place where animals took shelter, a small space to find safety from the wind and rain. Most liturgical churches today have a space called the narthex. A spiritual mudroom of sorts, it is a small space where a person is asked to leave their worldly cares behind before entering the sanctuary. God's presence can often be found where we feel safe.

Christ is often born in the small spaces.

Do you have a sacred space in your home? Can you find a quiet, private place to feel safe and to open your heart to God?

The Third Day
of Christmas
Baby

While they were there, the time came for her to deliver her child.

Luke 2:6

It is possible that the baby Jesus may have been premature. Mary walks or rides a donkey from Nazareth to Bethlehem, a distance of many miles. She is young. This is her first child. It is very possible that she delivers the baby early.

She does not eat much on the journey to Bethlehem—there are no convenience stores to satisfy the cravings of pregnant women. There are no prenatal vitamins or supplements. I'm sure Joseph carries all that he can on the long journey, but the rations are limited. Jesus is probably not a big baby, dimpled with cuddly legs. He is probably thin and small.

Mary and Joseph have no one but each other to help in the birth. Neither of them knows what they are doing. They must be so scared.

This tiny baby is born without a house or a doctor, to young parents who are frightened and alone. How strange for the All Powerful Maker of the Universe to come to us in this form.

When I was in college, I traveled to Russia to work in orphanages. One day, I visited a baby orphanage. A Russian woman told me that it was a sign of trust that I was even taken to the baby orphanage. *Not many Americans are allowed to see inside*, she said.

I have never forgotten what happened that day.

I went into a room filled with babies. Most of the babies were nearly silent, emitting only soft moans as they rocked themselves. I asked the woman why the babies were so quiet. And she explained: The babies stopped crying when they realized that no one was coming. They learned to comfort themselves.

But one little baby was crying hard. I rushed over to see what was wrong and picked her up.

She stopped crying immediately and looked at me with beautiful blue eyes and a watery smile.

You are the mother, the woman said. *Take her.*

But I was in college and the organization that I worked for did not allow us to try to adopt. I asked the woman to tell me about this little girl.

She was found in a garbage dumpster two days ago, the woman said. She still thinks that someone might come if she cries.

I left that day and did not go back. No one would take me to the orphanage. But I still remember the baby girl and the way she smiled at me.

Why would God come in such a helpless form? Can you picture holding the child Jesus? What does it mean to love God as we do a baby?

The Fourth Day of Christmas

Crying Baby

She…laid him in a manger.

Luke 2:7

When my boys cried at night, I bolted out of bed with urgency. What was wrong? What could I do? How could I help?

The cry of an infant is a sign that they need you, that they want to be held or they want you to look at them and be with them. It is a sign of the need to be loved.

I want you to think of God in a different way this Christmas. I want you to think of God as The Baby. I want you to realize that God cries out to you.

Many of us pray because we think it will help us, or we want God to help others. We think God will bring us more peace or understanding. But we are almost always driven to prayer because of our needs. We never stop to think that God might want us.

God chooses to become a child. God chooses to be born as the most dependent, small, helpless creature on the planet. God chooses to need us as a baby needs a mother, as a child needs to be held. God chooses you, and God cries out to you.

When you pray, go to God as you would go to hold a crying baby. Rush to God, without thinking or analyzing or wondering how much time you have: just run to God. God calls out to you. God has designed this creation in such a way that God is crying to you to come and be with him.

Remember the Garden of Eden? Remember how Adam and Eve ate the fruit of the Tree of the Knowledge of Good and Evil? And once they had eaten that fruit, they realized that they were naked, and they hid from God. They separated themselves from God first; they did the leaving. And God wandered in the Garden, calling to them. *Where are you?*

God has been searching for you ever since. The baby cries out to you to come and hold him; come and be with him.

It is strange to think of us holding God. It is strange to think of God wanting to be with us. But God longs for us, yearns for us, cries out for us. The All Powerful One, the Maker of the Universe chooses you. God makes you for a purpose. Just you. God wants you for exactly who you are.

The baby Jesus wants you, and he cries out to you tonight. He cries to you through the poor who don't have a place to sleep. He cries to you in the ill and those who are mourning. Jesus calls out for you to come to him, help him, minister to him and with him. *When you do anything for the least of these, you do it to me,* Jesus says. *I come among you as a baby who needs you.*

And this day, I call out to you. *Come back to me,* God says. *Come home.*

How do you hear God calling you through the needs of the world? How are you answering this call?

The Fifth Day
of Christmas
Born into Violence

When King Herod heard this, he was frightened, and all Jerusalem with him.

Matthew 2:3

Bashar al-Assad wants to hold on to his power as ruler of Syria. His family has been in power since 1971. He is willing to kill, maim, and displace thousands to secure his place in power. In December 2016, 40,000 people have been displaced within and around the area of Aleppo in Syria. Half are children.

Families are taken to the district of Jibreen where they have been given shelter in a large warehouse. The living conditions are bad, overcrowded, and freezing cold. Rain pours through holes in the roof and broken windows. Children huddle against their parents.

Is the world much different today than it was in the year that Christ was born? Technology has advanced. Medicine has advanced. But has the human soul advanced? Is there any real difference between Herod and Bashar al-Assad? Adult men are still sacrificing children for power and political gain. Violence is still rampant in the Middle East and in many parts of the world.

I have always wondered why God chooses to be born in the Middle East. Why would God choose to be born to refugees, to a homeless couple with no place to rest? Why not Australia, Canada, Sweden? Africa or the West Indies or America? There are so many beautiful and peaceful parts of the world. God must have made a conscious decision to be born in the midst of violence. Why?

When my father-in-law became sick with cancer, we could not believe it. This tall, strong, vibrant Methodist preacher with a full head of white hair looked invincible. How could he have cancer?

We took him to New York City for a second opinion. Surely he could lick this disease! If anyone could, he could.

I came back to the hotel one afternoon to find my husband and his dad standing in front of the mirror together. They were both shaving their heads.

My husband said words I will never forget. "I'm here with you, Dad," he said. "I am here."

The world was as broken and violent in first-century Bethlehem as it is today. And Jesus still comes to be with us, in this messed-up, frightening, violent, beautiful, chaotic, incredible world. He comes to be here, with you, with me.

I am here, God says. *I am here. I shave myself down to a tiny child so that I can be here with you.*

What does it mean to you that God chooses to be born into violence?

The Sixth Day
of Christmas
The Stars that Night

In that region there were shepherds living in the fields, keeping watch over their flock by night. Then an angel of the Lord stood before them, and the glory of the Lord shone around them, and they were terrified.

Luke 2:8-9

It is hot in Bethlehem, the hot that forces you to stay inside, under shelter during the heat of the day, only to emerge outside after the sun goes down. If you are a shepherd, trying to keep sheep alive, you pray for evening with its cooler temperatures and perhaps a breeze. The poor sheep are covered with wool, and no one wants to wear a wool coat on a blistering day.

The shepherds are used to the night shift. They sleep in caves or dwellings during the heat of the day and watch their flock at night. In the darkness, the shepherds learn the stars in their courses. They experience the resounding quiet of rolling hills and black skies, with nothing separating them from the heavens. These shepherds are used to a quiet life.

And then, one night, something extraordinary happens. Luke does not even try to tell us what it looks like, this celestial event. He calls it a multitude of the heavenly host. Do the stars merge into one great movement of light? Do thousands of angel wings cover the sky? Whatever it is, the experience is beyond anything the shepherds have ever seen. We know this because the shepherds respond with fear. Whatever appears in the sky this night is majestic enough to scare them silly.

Luke describes the event with the word glory: "And the glory of the Lord shone around them, and they were terrified." There is no adequate English word for *doxa*, the ancient Greek word that we translate as glory. It is a quality that is only used to describe the divine. It is used when Moses sees the backside of God on Mount Sinai. The same word is used throughout scripture when human beings are witnessing something otherworldly, something so magnificent that words are inadequate. The shepherds see something that defies explanation. And we have to be satisfied with the fact that they cannot describe the event. It is beyond words.

Have you ever experienced the glory of God? Could you find the right words to describe it?

The Seventh Day
of Christmas
The Name

*After eight days had passed, it was time to circumcise
the child; and he was called Jesus, the name given by
the angel before he was conceived in the womb.*

Luke 2:21

A few decades ago, the company Adidas sent two men to
Kenya to see if there was a viable market to sell sneakers
there. *Send a telegram back to us*, they said. *Let us know if
the market is good.*

The first man walked around Kenya for two weeks, then
sent this telegram: *Bad market here. No one wears shoes.*

The second man spent the same amount of time in the
country. He also sent a telegram. It read: *Great market
here. No one wears shoes!*

How do we choose to describe a place? What do we see? How do we speak about it? Our words have an impact on the world around us. We have the opportunity to name things—and we can decide if we name them through the lens of the first man or the second.

On the eighth day, Mary and Joseph circumcise the baby and give him a name. The Jews of Jesus' time wait until the eighth day to name a child, in part because so many babies die in infancy. Mary and Joseph call the baby Jesus because that is the name given to him by God through the angel. Jesus means *the One who saves.*

Throughout scripture, a hint of the essence of a person is contained within his or her name. When that person's essence is changed by God, his or her name also changes. For instance, Abram becomes Abraham, Jacob becomes Israel, and Saul becomes Paul. In this way, there is a hint of God's very essence in the name of Jesus. And when we utter that name, we reach out and touch that essence.

Human beings have the power to name. God gives Adam the power to name all the birds of the field and the fish of the sea. And God declares that they are good. We have the power to name ourselves and to name others. In this way, we carry a bit of God's nature within us. But we must wield this opportunity with much care: The power to name can be used for good or ill, to build up or tear down.

What you call yourself has power. Your name is holy too. Some names are not. Some names wound deeply. Have you used the power of naming for good—or have you on occasion abused the power?

The Eighth Day of Christmas

New Parents

When the time came for their purification according to the law of Moses, they brought him up to Jerusalem to present him to the Lord.

Luke 2:22

In Jesus' time, a woman is considered unclean for forty days after the birth of a child. Once the forty days are over, she and her husband are to take the child to the temple in Jerusalem, where they offer up a sacrifice of thanksgiving for the child. If they are rich, they are expected to sacrifice a lamb. If they are poor, they are asked to sacrifice two turtle doves or pigeons.

Mary and Joseph travel from Bethlehem to Jerusalem for this rite of purification. They offer two turtle doves and hold their newborn baby in their arms with the anxiety of young parents, wondering if they are doing okay, if the baby will be okay.

I remember taking our son Luke to a restaurant when he was just a few weeks old. We were so young and inexperienced that we left before even eating. We did not know how to keep him quiet or where to change him. We became so overwhelmed that we gave up and went home.

To step out into the world as a follower of Jesus is like being a new parent. How are we supposed to act? What are we supposed to say or do? What if someone asks us about our faith? What if someone asks us a question to which we don't know the answer? The life of faith changes everything, just like the birth of a child changes everything. And when you step out into the world as a changed person, you don't know exactly what will happen. Every interaction is altered, for now you live for God. The world is fresh and new and dangerous and frightening. And you will make it through, just as new parents navigate those early weeks, because Christ is with you, and Christ is love.

When you step out into the world, do you remember that you are first and foremost a follower of Christ? Does that make you open to new possibilities? Are you scared or excited (or both) about what God may do next in your life?

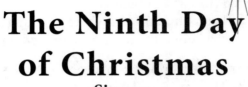

The Ninth Day
of Christmas
Simeon

*It had been revealed to [Simeon] by the Holy Spirit
that he would not see death before he had seen the
Lord's Messiah.*

Luke 2:26

Mary and Joseph are walking to the temple, scared and unsure
new parents, and then they see him. The old man. He walks up
to them with a look of intensity in his eyes. This is Simeon. God
has told him that he will not die until he sees the Messiah, the
Lord's anointed. And God tells him to go to worship that day.
And so there he is, looking all around, waiting for the Messiah.
We don't know how many years Simeon waited and watched,
but we know that he is still alive for this reason, to see Jesus.

Does Simeon know that the Messiah will be a baby? Is he
looking for a child?

We will never know the answer to those questions. But we know that Simeon comes to the temple expecting to see God's anointed one and he sees Jesus. He recognizes him.

There's a beautiful picture of the Dalai Lama. He is standing beside a metro car in a subway station. A baby boy is in his mother's arms and seated inside the car. The baby is leaning into the window, smiling at the Dalai Lama and the Dalai Lama has his hand to the window, with this playful look of anticipation and joy on his face, as if he has never seen anything more beautiful than that child.

"Now, I can die," Simeon says, "for I have seen this child."

Simeon comes to the temple expecting to see God.

Why did you read this meditation today? Did you attend church this week? In either of those experiences, did you expect to see God? Did you expect to have your life changed, to catch a glimpse of God's will for your life? Simeon not only prays deeply, but he takes the next step in a life of prayer, the courageous step that most of us are terrified to take. After he prays, he expects and waits for God's promise.

Too often we dare not expect so much of God. What would happen if we approached each day with the same prayerful reverence and watchful expectation as Simeon?

Why do you come to church? What are you hoping to find? If you do not name your hopes and dreams and desires to God, how will you know when you have been heard or your prayers answered?

The Tenth Day of Christmas
Wise

Wise men from the East came to Jerusalem, asking, "Where is the child who has been born king of the Jews? For we observed his star at its rising, and have come to pay him homage."

Matthew 2:1-2

We do not know for sure the number of Wise Men. It is unlikely that they were kings, although they did bring gifts fit for a king. A lot of folklore surrounds the story. What the gospels actually say is that they came from the east, and they were wise. There could have been two, or four, or fifty of them. They brought gifts fit for a king: three gifts to be precise, which is why we assume that there were three of them. They brought gold, frankincense, and myrrh. That's all we know.

The only adjective used to describe these men is the word wise. They are wise.

What does it mean to be wise? How can you and I be wise? The implication is that the wisdom of the men enables them to find Jesus. I want to be wise so I can find Christ too.

Let's look at what these wise men do: They watch the skies. They live in the present moment, asking themselves: *What is God doing now?* Their awareness and their attention to the skies help them to see Christ. Their wisdom has nothing to do with knowledge; it has to do with awareness, with the ability to listen.

Have you ever spoken to a sailor who has navigated by the stars? It is rarely done these days. Following the stars means constant vigilance. There are no other landmarks. You must constantly place yourself in reference to the cosmic event that you are observing. You are in a living and moving relationship with the stars, for your place with them is ever shifting and changing. You cannot fall asleep. You must keep your eyes open. You must become part of the cosmic dance.

To be wise means to be fully awake, to watch and listen for God's movement in the world. When have you been most awake?

The Eleventh Day
of Christmas
The Wisdom of Gratitude

On entering the house, they saw the child with Mary his mother; and they knelt down and paid him homage.

Matthew 2:11

We have a parishioner who has been given a difficult diagnosis. Doctors say Ken has a rare brain disease and predict he will live for about six months. So we are praying for a miracle. Ken wants me to ask you to join us in praying. So far, he seems to be defying all the expectations of the doctors.

Another miracle has happened to Ken and to his wife Sharon in this period. They have become wise. You see, this diagnosis has pushed Ken to live in the present moment. He cherishes every single thing: the beautiful sky outside his house, his granddaughters' artwork, his music. He is alive and present, more than ever before. We do not know what God will do in Ken's life, but we know that one prayer has already been answered. Ken is awake. He is teaching us how to live and how to talk to people about God. Ken is grateful for each moment.

They say that in the time of the birth of Jesus, three stars merged to create a cosmic event that was spectacular. It makes me wonder. Why didn't huge populations of people leave their homes and follow the magnificent light show? Why weren't Mary, Joseph, and baby Jesus inundated with throngs of people? So many people failed to notice the sky—or understand what it meant.

In an old Indian folk tale, a man runs from a tiger. The tiger chases him, and the man runs off a precipice. As he is falling down, the man grabs hold of the roots of a tree. He holds on for dear life and looks up to see the tiger pacing and growling above him. He looks down to see a cobra slithering and hissing in the grass below. He looks at the tree roots and notices a small mouse is nibbling at the roots. And right above him, hanging on a branch, is a honeycomb. The honey drips onto the back of his hand. The man licks the honey, and it is so sweet.

This is the story of our lives. Our past is the tiger, who hunts us down and paces, hoping to seize our minds and devour them with all the mistakes we have made or with a voracious longing for the way things were. The future is the cobra, who slithers around waiting to wrap us up in fears and hopes and plans for tomorrow. Even the present moment is nibbled away by the mouse. But in the now, the sweetness of God is available for us to savor. It comes to us as a free gift, sweet and rare and beautiful. It is up to us to taste it and give thanks.

The greatest way to wisdom is to give thanks. The wise men gave thanks and gave generously of their belongings. How can you be wise enough to give?

The Twelfth Day
of Christmas
The Move

Then Joseph got up, took the child and his mother by night, and went to Egypt.

Matthew 2:14

Human beings are perpetually in motion. When I became pregnant with my son, I wanted to be planted, rooted. Like many parents, I prepared a nursery and nested. It seemed safer to have a baby in one place, to keep that baby planted in time and space. But it is impossible.

The Bible is a story of humans on the move, from the expulsion from Eden to the journey toward heaven. The Hebrew people must leave slavery to grow into a full relationship with God. Jesus is constantly on the move as an adult. When he calls his disciples, he tells them to follow him. He does not say, *Come and stay with me.* No, Jesus is always on the move.

It is no surprise that as a baby, Jesus must also move. His father and mother must move to Bethlehem to be counted, then they must flee to Egypt to protect the baby from the paranoia and death threats of Herod. Jesus, the Incarnation of God, has to move as soon as he is born.

To be alive is to be on the move. It is the only way to find God, to move with the power of the Holy Spirit—to keep on moving and changing and growing. Human life is movement—even our cells change and grow. God in Christ lets us know that this constant state of motion is okay. It is even holy. We are meant to move and change and grow. There is really no permanent home for any of us here. There is no room for any of us. We don't really belong here and neither does Jesus. We belong to another land, a land of true milk and honey, our true home.

Yesterday, I prayed with a woman who is dying. She is blind and bedridden. But her smile was wide and beautiful. "I am ready to go home," she said.

Christian author Brian McLaren writes in his book *The Great Spiritual Migration*: "I've come to see that what matters most is not our status but our trajectory, not where we are but where we we're going, not where we stand but where we are headed. Christian faith for me is no longer a static location but a great spiritual journey. And that changes everything."

As a human being, you are moving. Where are you headed?

Conclusion
Coming in Deeper

I love to read stories over and over again. My family will make fun of me when I pick up a novel that I have read ten times already! But the more familiar the story, the deeper I can move into the plot, the safer I feel to explore the details.

The story of the birth of Jesus is told in only two of the four gospels. And those two gospels recount Jesus' birth in entirely different ways. In Matthew, we hear of Joseph's dreams and the devotion of Wise Men. In Luke, we learn of Mary and her cousin Elizabeth, babies leaping in wombs, angels appearing, and shepherds becoming frightened. How can the two gospels tell such different stories about the same event?

For Matthew, the lineage of the Messiah reaching back to King David is an essential message. Joseph represents the bloodline that is so sacred, so full of hope and redemption. For Luke, the essential message is the story of the faithful women who agree to birth children for God. Mary and Elizabeth, then, are the pivotal characters in Luke's telling.

When you enter a story, you bring your own unique perspective. You begin to understand how God has given you insights that perhaps no one else has. You can look into the story and see inside yourself.

Keep reading, keep listening, keep learning. The story of Christ's birth can be both familiar and new in each re-telling. Come and see.

About the Author

Katherine B. (Kate) Moorehead is the tenth dean of St. John's Episcopal Cathedral in Jacksonville, Florida. As dean, Kate serves as vice president of the Episcopal School of Jacksonville, the Cathedral School Early Learning Center, the Cathedral Arts Project, the CathedralCare nursing facility, and Aging True Community Senior Services, all nonprofits birthed from the cathedral. Kate graduated Phi Beta Kappa from Vassar College and graduated cum laude with a Master of Divinity degree from Virginia Theological Seminary. She is the author of five books, including *Get Over Yourself: God's Here, Resurrecting Easter,* and *Healed: The Truth about Mary Magdalene.* Kate and her husband, James (J.D.), have three sons, Luke, Jake, and Max.

About Forward Movement

Forward Movement is committed to inspiring disciples and empowering evangelists. While we produce great resources like this book, Forward Movement is not a publishing company. We are a ministry. Publishing books, daily reflections, studies for small groups, and online resources are important ways that we live out this ministry. More than a half million people read our daily devotions through *Forward Day by Day*, which is also available in Spanish (*Adelante Día a Día*) and Braille, online, as a podcast, and as an app for your smartphones or tablets. It is mailed to more than fifty countries, and we donate nearly 30,000 copies each quarter to prisons, hospitals, and nursing homes. We actively seek partners across the Church and look for ways to provide resources that inspire and challenge. A ministry of the Episcopal Church for eighty years, Forward Movement is a nonprofit organization funded by sales of resources and gifts from generous donors.

To learn more about Forward Movement and our resources, visit www.ForwardMovement.org or www.VenAdelante.org. We are delighted to be doing this work and invite your prayers and support.